Original title:
The Ghosts of What We Were

Copyright © 2024 Creative Arts Management OÜ
All rights reserved.

Author: Violet Murphy
ISBN HARDBACK: 978-9908-0-0622-2
ISBN PAPERBACK: 978-9908-0-0623-9

Footsteps that Fade into Silence

In the attic, old hats once worn,
Dance with dreams that feel so torn.
A sock puppet sings a silly tune,
While we laugh at shadows under the moon.

In corners where dust bunnies play,
Whispers of mischief in disarray.
A chair creaks, pretending to sway,
As memories trip in a funny ballet.

Forgotten crayons scribble the past,
Drawing wild stories that fly by fast.
A rubber chicken sits with pride,
In this theater of whims, we all reside.

Beneath the stairs, old jokes reside,
They chuckle along, no place to hide.
In laughter, we find our playful song,
As footsteps fade, but the fun goes on.

Fragments of Love's Last Breath

In a cupboard, old socks lay,
Forgotten gifts from yesterday.
With a sigh, the memories peek,
All the laughter, now just meek.

A card of hearts, a crumpled joke,
Eras of bliss wrapped in a yoke.
Love's big bloom now a wilted plant,
Each petal whispers, 'I just can't.'

Eclipsed by Time's Embrace

Once we danced like feathered birds,
Now we shuffle, misheard words.
Chasing the youth like a bad dream,
Wobbly knees, but still we beam.

Photos fade, the colors blur,
That hairstyle? Oh, what a fur!
Time chuckles, the clock's a tease,
While we try to squeeze into these.

Remnants of Unwritten Songs

An old guitar with just one string,
The chords of life, how they still cling.
We strum a note and laugh aloud,
As melodies drift through the crowd.

Scribbled lyrics on a napkin,
'What rhymes with fun?' my brain's a mappin'.
But laughs like these need not a score,
For friendship's tune, we need no more.

When Time Stood Still

A pair of shoes, two lefts, not right,
Once danced away in the soft moonlight.
Now they sit, telling tales of woe,
Of vibrant nights and a distant show.

We waited for life, but it skipped a beat,
Now stories age like a chunk of meat.
With every tick, our laughter's sealed,
In the tapestry of time, we're knee-deep healed.

Remnants of Unspoken Dreams

In a box of forgotten toys,
Dust bunnies gather like old boys.
A yo-yo spins with a creaky grin,
Whispering tales of where we've been.

A shoebox packed with crumpled dreams,
Just paper boats lost in wild streams.
Pillow forts that stood with pride,
Now sag with secrets they can't hide.

Haunting Echoes of Yesterday

The swing set sways with the ghost of glee,
An empty slide calls out quietly.
Laughter lingers in creaky swings,
While shadows dance on imaginary wings.

Chasing memories like a lost kite,
Stuck in a tree, what a silly sight!
Tea parties held with a stuffed bear host,
We toasted to dreams we now love the most.

Reflections in a Dusty Mirror

In cracks of glass, we find our youth,
A timid grin, a lost-tooth truth.
Pigtails flail in a ghostly breeze,
As we strike silly poses with ease.

A clumsy dance in the bathroom light,
Our shadows giggle, what a delight!
Every smudge tells a story bold,
Of prankster dreams we still hold.

Specters of Childhood Laughter

Under the bed, those socks conspire,
They tiptoe out, plotting to retire.
Cartwheels echo in the autumn leaves,
As silly whispers float on the eaves.

Hide-and-seek with a ghostly flair,
We'd vanish quick, not a single care.
Giggling memories, so light and free,
Chasing shadows like a wild spree.

The Unseen Letters from the Past

In a drawer full of secrets, they lie,
A love note from someone, oh my!
With ink smudged and a heart that won't quit,
It's like reading a comic, a comedic skit.

A shopping list scribbled with flair,
"Dear John, please buy cheese and some air!"
Ghostly reminders of times long gone,
Still make me chuckle with each silly con.

Fragments of Yesterday's Light

The sunbeams dance through the old frames,
Shadows whispering forgotten names.
A sock puppet show puts us in stitches,
While misfit toys share their double-itches.

We laughed at our hairstyles, so grand,
Big enough to form a small band.
Yet here we are, kept safe in time,
Like jumbled lyrics of a jester's rhyme.

When Time Whispered Our Names

Time wore a tutu, oh what a sight,
Twisting and twirling in the pale moonlight.
Ticking away with a wink and a grin,
While we danced like we'd never begin.

Slippers and socks with holes, quite a pair,
Marathon runners could use some flair.
Dreams woven like yarn flung from a cat,
Chasing after memories, much like that.

Photographs in a Dusty Album

Snapshots trapped in a cobwebbed nest,
My Uncle Joe dressed up like a quest.
The dog photobombed every single shot,
With a goofy grin, he stole the plot.

Stains on the pages tell tales of cake,
Each birthday party, a wide-eyed wake.
We're still laughing with our photogenic fate,
Thanks to the laughter we call our great mate.

Lost Letters from a Distant Past

In an attic, dusty tales lay,
Forgotten words that meant to play.
With ink that smudged and dreams so wild,
I laugh at letters, lost, reviled.

A note from Soggy Sock, my mate,
Claimed tater tots could seal our fate.
In crayon scrawls adorned with cheer,
They spoke of snacks, not shedding tears.

Each paper whisper, a giggle fit,
Of how we thought we'd never quit.
Yet time has taken quite a toll,
Now I bake cookies, eat the whole bowl.

Those letters, silly and quite absurd,
Remind me of the dreams unheard.
As laughter echoes through the hall,
I cherish each scribbled, forgotten scrawl.

Letters Written in the Wind

The breeze carries whispers of old,
Where secrets of youth were once bold.
Tickling leaves with a playful grin,
I hear tales of when we'd begin.

A letter glanced off a tree so high,
Said 'Beware of pies that can fly!'
With giggles shared under the sun,
Oh, how we thought life was just fun.

The wind knows more than we can say,
Ballet of breezes in childlike play.
It swirls around with a jesting tune,
Recalling sprites dancing 'neath the moon.

These letters dance, they twist and sway,
Like my dreams that once went astray.
In every gust that tickles my face,
I find laughter in our wild chase.

The Silence Between Us

A pause hangs thick as buttered toast,
It's in this silence where I can boast.
Like socks unmatched and jokes that flop,
We embrace the hush, let giggles pop.

When words once flowed like soda spouts,
Now we nibble on what life's about.
Between the quiet, a joke lays low,
Pending the punchline, just for show.

The silence dips in a whimsical groove,
A dance unplanned, yet we still move.
In glances shared, the laughter squeaks,
As time unwinds, the humor peaks.

So let us savor this quiet embrace,
Where chuckles bloom in our own space.
The silence feels like a warm old friend,
With every giggle, we start to mend.

Ghostly Footprints on the Shore

Footprints washed away by a playful tide,
What secrets do they hold, where do they hide?
Each print a story, a laughter shared,
Of silly pranks when no one cared.

A sandcastle grand, now a mere trace,
With jellyfish tossing a wobbly race.
I chased seagulls thinking I'd fly,
But they laughed at me as they passed by.

Whispers of surf, a spirited cheer,
Through salty air, the jokes still appear.
Shells giggle softly, their secrets keep,
As they echo softly, making me leap.

Each ghostly mark tells tales so fleet,
Of days in sunshine, where joy was sweet.
With every wave that breaks at dawn,
I find the laughter still lingers on.

The Remnant of Our Togetherness

We once danced like two silly geese,
Eating cake amidst the chaos,
Now we trip on memories sweet,
With frosting clues held aloft.

Laughter echoes in the hall,
As we wear mismatched socks,
Forgotten romance in the aisle,
Pineapple on pizza, who knocks?

Every joke was pure delight,
Like juggling cats in the night,
Now we just chuckle and sigh,
Two old friends who still rely.

Our photos flicker, yet we grin,
Sharing tales of our antics,
In every glance, a mischievous win,
A comedic love, the best of tricks.

Flickering Lanterns on an Old Path

Once we twinkled like fireflies,
Guiding each other through the dark,
Now we stumble on old sighs,
Trip over dreams, miss the mark.

Lanterns sway in the dusky air,
As shadows dance with silly grace,
We laugh at our past and dare,
To weave our steps in a crazy race.

Recollections bloom like wildflowers,
Remember that time we sang?
All the neighbors looked so sour,
But in our hearts, the joy would clang.

Amidst the laughter and shared thoughts,
Whispers of 'what if?' now roam,
Flickering light in tangled knots,
A trail of banter, our strange home.

When the Seasons Forgot Us

When winter wore a parka too tight,
And summer arrived with a frown,
We made hats from our old laundry,
As the seasons melted down.

With sweaters as capes in the heat,
We danced with the wind, oh so free,
While autumn threw leaves at our feet,
We giggled like children, you and me.

Spring knocked but forgot to bring bloom,
Instead, we plucked daisies on cue,
Our playful hearts filled up the room,
As nature forgot what to do.

The calendar flipped, what a mess,
Time's prank beckoned our allure,
Yet in this chaos, found no stress,
For laughter was always the cure.

Echoes Across the Empty Rooms

In these hollow halls, our laughter bounced,
   Off walls that held secrets and cheer,
   Echoes giggle, like they announced,
  Our youthful follies, still quite near.

We wore mismatched shoes then, so bold,
   And danced madly in the living room,
   Memories wrapped in threads of gold,
While dust bunnies cheered every boom!

  With each empty room, a tale unfolds,
   Of socks thrown in games of delight,
   Candy wrappers that time now holds,
  Like whispers that linger in the night.

  Though chairs sit silent, we still sway,
  In rhythm with the past's sweet song,
   Echoes remind us, come what may,
    Together we've always belonged.

Etched in the Canvas of Memory

Once we danced with socks on our feet,
Spinning tales with a bowl of cold beet.
Laughed till we cried, the universe spun,
Chasing mischief, oh what fun!

Wearing capes made of sheets, quite the sight,
Pretending we soared in the moonlight.
Mischief in the air, sugar on hand,
We were heroes in our fairyland.

Birthday cakes that never were baked,
Ideas so wild, logic forsaked.
We penned our lives on the walls,
With crayons and giggles, the laughter calls.

And now we smile at the past we've spun,
Wondering where all those moments have run.
In the gallery of life, a quirky display,
Painted with laughter, come what may.

Shadows Cast by Fleeting Joy

In a world of aprons covered with stains,
We crafted wonders, ignoring the pains.
Juggling doughnuts while slipping on ice,
Each mishap a gem, oh so precise.

Fart jokes flew like confetti in air,
Laughter erupted, no room for despair.
Our inside jokes, a secretive band,
Echoing softly, a quirky stand.

Under the table, we'd giggle and hide,
While the grown-ups debated and pried.
Those silly moments, a fleeting mirage,
Yet in our hearts, they're a grand collage.

Shadows may play on the walls of our time,
Yet the laughter we shared is forever sublime.
So here's to the joy we can still recall,
A masquerade of memories, the best of all.

A Tapestry of Lost Whispers

Whispers of joy woven with glee,
In a land where we roamed wild and free.
Tea parties with mud, how quaintly absurd,
Each sip a giggle, every bite a word.

We built castles from pillows so grand,
With guardians of fluff that took a strong stand.
Each blanket a ship that sailed to delight,
Charting stars in our imaginations at night.

We traded our marbles for stories untold,
Creating a world worth far more than gold.
Nature's confetti sprinkled in air,
Dancing with echoes that shimmer with flair.

Now memories linger like fairies in flight,
Twinkling in silence, enchanting the night.
Though time drifts by on its whimsical quest,
In our hearts, those whispers forever rest.

Threads of Time Unspooled

With threads of laughter, we stitched our dreams,
In a realm where nothing is as it seems.
Playing hide and seek in shadows so tall,
Catching sweet whispers, we'd never fall.

We penned our tales in jellybean hues,
Sailing on clouds, with nothing to lose.
The time we stole, oh, what a delight,
With giggles that danced in the soft moonlight.

Candy-coated schemes and reckless flair,
Tickles and tumbles, we didn't have a care.
We spun wildly, left ghosts in our wake,
In the scrapbook of time, joy we did make.

Now as we ponder the fabric of days,
Threads unravel, life's whimsical ways.
Yet the laughter remains, spun oh so bright,
In the tapestry woven of sheer delight.

Glimpses of an Illusive Dream

Once we danced like wild spry things,
Chasing shadows, giggling at kings.
With socks on our feet, we'd trip and fall,
Collecting the crumbs from the midnight call.

A sandwich in hand, we'd plot world fame,
While dogs barked loudly, playing our game.
Oh, the plans we concocted grew big like balloons,
Till reality popped them, much like cartoon tunes.

Our secrets whispered, under moon's glow,
As the fridge door creaked with snacks on show.
We pranced in pajamas, a hilarious sight,
Summoning laughter deep into the night.

Now we sit and recall with smiles and sighs,
Those crazy adventures, truth wrapped in lies.
Though days have flown like feathers on air,
We keep those jokes safe, forever to share.

A Celestial Memoir of Silence.

In the attic, dust bunnies dance and sway,
With old records spinning, they steal the day.
Each note a whisper of what's gone by,
A cosmic comedy, making us sigh.

We dressed up as pirates with cardboard swords,
Raiding the pantry, eating our hoards.
The cat was our captain, regal and proud,
We laughed till we cried, shouting out loud.

Underneath the blanket fort, dreams took flight,
With a flashlight glowing, we shone so bright.
Tales of adventures on Mars and the moon,
A spaceship made of pillows, launching with tune.

Yet here we are, sipping our tea,
With memories of laughter, wild and free.
Though time may have passed like a trickster's game,
We cherish those moments, forever the same.

Echoes of Broken Dreams

Once we were astronauts heading to space,
Trading our homework for zero-gravity race.
In searching for stars, we forgot our math,
But laughter was sturdy, guiding our path.

Climbing trees, we'd claim a kingdom high,
Using swings as chariots, we'd touch the sky.
With kites that soared, and sandwiches shared,
In a world of make-believe, we boldly dared.

The echoes of giggles haunt parks where we played,
In superhero capes, our fears would evade.
Yet time slipped away, like sand through hands,
Our adventures now mere footprints in lands.

But we still smile, when shadows draw near,
Remembering moments that spark up our cheer.
In a treasure chest filled with bittersweet schemes,
We find the essence of all our bright dreams.

Shadows of Forgotten Laughter

In an old photo book, we peek and we grin,
Barrel full of laughs, where all tales begin.
With ice cream mustaches, we posed with flair,
Hoping to capture the sun in our hair.

We fished for wishes in puddles of rain,
Boys turned to frogs, who then danced in pain.
Whispering secrets to trees standing tall,
Our giggles a potion, enchanting us all.

Rolling down hills, we'd tumble and clash,
Each bruise a badge, a memory to stash.
In games of pretend where we'd boldly claim,
The world was our stage, a raucous, wild name.

Now those moments flutter like leaves in the breeze,
Tucking them gently in memories' freeze.
With shadows of laughter, we'll always remain,
As echoes of joy sprinkle life with sweet rain.

Embracing the Wistful Winds

Whispers dance like leaves in fall,
Once bright colors now seem small.
We laugh at tales of our old mistakes,
As if time swore, that's how it makes.

We prance through shadows of what we knew,
In mismatched socks, a comical view.
The past, a jester with tricks so sly,
Making us chuckle as seconds fly.

Remembering antics like silly hats,
We wear on our heads, like garden rats.
Once full of swagger, now a bit bent,
Yet laughter lingers; it's heaven-sent.

So here we sway in memory's tide,
With silly grins that we can't hide.
Let's toast to time, with glasses raised high,
For life's a hoot and we can't deny.

Flickers of Time's Erosion

Tick-tock giggles, oh what a sound,
As moments tumble all around.
We trip and fall on our old delight,
Chasing shadows in funny light.

The clock's a prankster, pulling strings tight,
Snickering softly in the dead of night.
We flirt with fate in our ragged cheer,
Playing dress-up with our yesteryear.

Wobbling on memory's fragile beam,
Like jelly beans, we squish and scream.
Laugh lines deepen like creased-up maps,
We smile at time and all its mishaps.

So here's to the whims and fancies spun,
Life's a laugh, and we're having fun.
In a frolic, through tickling time's grimace,
We find the jesters in every place.

The Fade of Lively Moments

Moments drift like kites in the breeze,
Each whimsy floats, teasing with ease.
We jumble our dreams like puzzle pieces,
Chasing lost laughter as fun never ceases.

With ticklish thoughts of days gone by,
We giggle at ghosts 'neath the twilight sky.
Flatulent echoes from deep in the past,
Bring chuckles and snorts that forever last.

Lively moments now in a soft rewind,
Twisting and turning, oh how they're twined.
Old photos grin like old friends might do,
Past is a party, come join us too!

So raise the chorus, let laughter prevail,
For time is a jokester; it loves to regale.
In the dance with old tales, let's merge and bend,
The faded giggles we never can end.

Unraveled Threads of Time

Threads unravel, a whimsical mess,
Stitching our lives into giggly dress.
Fuzzy memories twirl like dervishes,
We can't help but laugh at our past wishes.

In the fabric of time, we stitch in delight,
Twirls and whirls make the old seem bright.
With puffs of laughter, the air fills with mirth,
Celebrating the chaos of our worth.

Silly antics flash like neon signs,
A slapstick show where nothing aligns.
We juggle with memories like clowns with pie,
Enjoying the messes, oh how we fly!

Cheers to the moments, every twist and turn,
In the kite of our lives, for laughter we yearn.
As time shifts and twists, let joy be the theme,
In every faux pas, we weave a dream.

Stories Etched in Dust

In the attic, old hats hid,
With secrets they always slid.
A musty tome, full of glee,
It spills tales of a bumblebee.

Shoes that danced on floors of yore,
Now they just gather more and more.
A sock puppet, a lonely friend,
Wishing for a story to mend.

Time's playful chair rocks and creaks,
As the vintage clock tickles and sneaks.
Silly socks in a drawer's abyss,
Chasing memories that giggle and hiss.

So let's sip tea on this old rug,
And laugh at past's aging hug.
Dust holds smiles, not just a fuss,
A whimsical world waiting for us.

Echoes of Abandoned Roads

Down the lane where toys decay,
A skateboard hides, all chippy and gray.
Rusty bikes, perfect for a ride,
With hopes of a dragon to glide.

Puddles reflect a clown's last show,
With shoes so big, they steal the glow.
Forgotten pranks on every street,
Echo laughter that can't be beat.

Old tires roll in circles' dance,
Telling tales of misfit romance.
Ghosts of picnics under the sun,
Where lemonade was always fun.

So here's to paths that we avoid,
With whispers of joy, never destroyed.
Let's wander where the echoes play,
And bring back the smiles of yesterday.

Where Time Slumbered

In a nook where memories nap,
A radio plays an old-time clap.
Through velvet curtains, sunlight peeks,
Awakening laughter from shadowed weeks.

Old games call in a voice so soft,
Inviting dreams to float and loft.
A rubber ball with patches worn,
Shares stories of innocence reborn.

Worn-out slippers by the bedside,
Wish for adventures, undenied.
A teddy bear with a missing ear,
Sighs with secrets, loud and clear.

So let's tiptoe through this space,
Join the fun of a bygone race.
Time's held close in quilted threads,
Where slumbering joy never dreads.

Tattered Threads of a Tainted Past

In the corner, an ugly rug,
Holds the giggles of a playful bug.
A quilt made of dreams and stains,
Tells tales of sunshine and rains.

Old coats hang with buttons shy,
As if to wink and wave goodbye.
Mismatched mittens dance in pairs,
Chasing shadows, spinning cares.

A lunchbox with candy, half-eaten,
Recalls days of a child's sweet greeting.
With every crumb, a smile is found,
In the messiness of joy unbound.

So let's rummage through this pile,
And find the one that makes us smile.
Though tattered threads might hold some past,
They weave the funny shadows that last.

Memories in the Mist

In the attic, dusty hats,
A clown wig, and tennis bats.
Where laughter echoes down the hall,
And silly monologues recall.

We danced in our mismatched shoes,
Underneath a fuchsia moon's hues.
We tried to juggle hopes and dreams,
But ended up just busting seams.

A prank call from a phantom friend,
The punchline never seems to end.
With party hats and cake so old,
Our antics are a sight to behold.

Those days were jokes we couldn't quit,
Ghosts in costumes all misfit.
Yet here we stand, a merry band,
With smiles as bright as desert sand.

Phantoms of Yesterday's Joy

We chased our dreams on squeaky bikes,
Played hide and seek with ghoulish spikes.
With capes made of sheets, we were bold,
Our laughter rang out pure as gold.

In baseball caps and smiling grins,
We sang of adventures, mischievous sins.
Each shadow held a tale to tell,
Of playful pranks that went so well.

Dancing shadows in the park,
Comedic poses till it's dark.
With giggles caught in twilight's breath,
We toyed with time, we're not done yet.

So toast to phantoms, loud and proud,
To the crazy moments we've avowed.
A colorful gallery of who we've been,
In every memory, we still grin.

Haunting Remnants of Us

A broken kite stuck in the tree,
A remnant of our glee, you see?
With feathers and strings all tangled tight,
We laughed, embracing such a sight.

A treasure chest filled with old toys,
Echoes of our childish joys.
Plastic gadgets and silly hats,
Recalling freeze tag and playful spats.

The garden's full of dreams we dug,
Where secret laughs and friendships tug.
Each swing a ghost of countless plays,
Our hearts in laughter still ablaze.

Let's raise a glass to silly schemes,
To family feuds and shattered dreams.
For in the echoes of the past,
We dance around joy's shadow cast.

Silhouettes of What Could Have Been

In a world where we wore capes,
We dreamed of magic, making escapes.
With cardboard swords and grand charades,
The silly tales that we paraded.

Collecting secrets on the run,
Imaginary battles all in fun.
We wrote our names in cosmic dust,
And fibbed about our brave trust.

Every corner held a new surprise,
Tickles, giggles, and playful lies.
As silhouettes danced against the snack,
Wonders piled high, no looking back.

So here's to laughter, loud and bright,
To memories echoing, a pure delight.
For in the theater of our past,
We find the joy that's meant to last.

Echoes of Lost Tomorrows

We danced in socks on wooden floors,
Chased our dreams outside of doors.
With silly hats and wild applause,
We laughed until we lost our drawers.

Oh, that time we tried to bake a pie,
It turned out flat, a lopsided fry.
We buried it with a solemn fuss,
Now it's a legend, just us and the crust.

Bubblegum bursts and skateboard falls,
Eraser fights in echoing halls.
Yet every chuckle, every cheer,
Is, somehow, still so crystal clear.

Whispers from Forgotten Memories

Remember when we wore our shoes,
On the wrong feet, just to amuse?
The world spun 'round, we felt so bold,
With tales so ridiculous, they never get old.

We peered out through the schoolyard gate,
Imagining our future fate.
We thought we'd fly, not merely run,
Instead, we tripped—still had our fun!

We built castles made of cheese,
Argued fiercely with honeybees.
Though those days seem far away,
We still chuckle with kids today.

Shadows of Laughter Past

A paper plane took flight and soared,
But landed right where Dad snored.
We giggled as it hit the floor,
He woke up puzzled, "What's in store?"

We captured fireflies in a jar,
Tried to race our bikes so far.
But crashing down, we lost the race,
With mud and grass all over our face.

Now as we sit and reminisce,
We laugh at every playful miss.
In shadows where our laughter played,
The echoes of our youth won't fade.

Fragments of Faded Days

Once we tried to ride a goat,
Thought we could steer it, not just float.
It took off fast like it was right,
Turned our picnic into a fright!

Sock puppets squeaked at puppet shows,
Spilling secrets that nobody knows.
We'd plan our heists with wink and nod,
But hid the evidence in Dad's car marred.

Each fragment of those foolish dreams,
A tapestry woven with laughter screams.
Though years have passed, the joy remains,
In simple doodles and silly refrains.

Lingering Elegies of Time

In closets old, my socks have wed,
They dance alone in dreams instead.
The mugs once filled now gather dust,
Their laughter echoed, lost in rust.

Old chairs complain with every weight,
They grumble like an aging mate.
While photos grin from yellowed frames,
Reminding me of silly games.

The garden gnomes plot mischief near,
While crickets tap their raucous cheer.
We once were spry, now we just wheeze,
Chasing shadows in a gentle breeze.

Yet as I laugh with every thought,
I treasure ghosts that joy has brought.
For every whim that's left behind,
Reminds me of what's intertwined.

Traces of Vanished Moments

The pie I baked went up in flames,
And now my kitchen tells me names.
The spatula, a spoon saw it too,
Their stories linger, bold and true.

My phone's full of photos, oh so clear,
Of faces I can barely bear.
Smiles that faded like my socks,
Found in places they shouldn't dock.

The cat just stares at our old chair,
As if it knows our past affair.
How we once danced like no one's there,
Now it rolls its eyes, just doesn't care.

Yet in the chatter of the clock,
I hear the giggles, feel the shock.
For moments lost become the jests,
That tickle time and all the rests.

The Shadowplay of What Once Was

Back in the day, I had great hair,
Now wind just laughs, it's not so fair.
My old cologne still haunts the hall,
A ghostly scent, I guess, that's all.

The fridge, it hums a lowly tune,
While leftovers take on shapes like moons.
They whisper tales of what we'd eat,
Amassing flavor, fading sweet.

Old shoes lie crumpled by the door,
They claim they danced, but who's keeping score?
Each scuffed report of happy trails,
Now resembles fishy, twisted tales.

With laughter lingering through the air,
I toast to memories, bold and rare.
For every moment that's gone awry,
Brings warmth that makes the heart comply.

Crumbling Castles of Memory

The lawn gnome reigns on mossy throne,
Guarding secrets it has outgrown.
While marbles roll like dreams in flight,
They chuckle softly through the night.

Old bikes lie rusting by the fence,
Once racing dreams that felt so tense.
They squeak out tales of distant rides,
As wind whispers where fun abides.

The old porch swing sways without rhyme,
Collecting stories lost in time.
With creaks and groans, it holds its sway,
Recalling laughter from yesterday.

Yet here I stand, absurdly glad,
For crumbling castles can't feel sad.
In every laugh, a treasure mound,
Of remnants sweet, forever found.

The Tides of Our Reminiscence

Waves of laughter crash and play,
Silly moments, bright as day.
We danced like fools, forgot the time,
Now we giggle at our prime.

With each tide, a memory floats,
Bizarre tales that makes us gloat.
Who thought that trip would go awry?
A mudslide chase, oh my, oh my!

Friendship forged in curious ways,
Like that time we lost our gaze.
Fishing hats flew, winds did conspire,
And all we caught was that strange quire.

So here we stand, at ocean's edge,
Waving to ghosts, we'll make a pledge.
To laugh at those wild days gone by,
As tides shift low and laughter high.

Faded Pages of a Shared Story

Dusty books on a shelf so high,
Each tale makes us laugh, oh my!
A recipe for disaster here,
Burnt pancakes, our greatest fear.

Flip the pages, whispers of fun,
Pranks and laughs, oh, we've just begun!
Caught up in plots, like untrained mice,
Knocking over stuff, oh, isn't that nice?

Characters strange, with wigs askew,
Dramatic flair for the absurd crew.
Our acting? A comical sight,
Bowing down, we'd laugh till night.

So pen these tales with a chuckle loud,
We were the odd ones, we were the proud.
Faded pages with stories sweet,
Our memories, a glorious feat.

Echoes in the Halls of Memory

Whispers hark from walls once bright,
Echoing laughter, pure delight.
Sock puppet shows, a grand charade,
Fuzzy red hair, an odd parade.

In halls where we once feigned our charm,
Spilling secrets, causing alarm.
A slip, a trip, we'd laugh till we cried,
Now echoes linger, fun amplified.

Our dance-offs, pure clumsy grace,
Each step a silly, frantic race.
From here to there, not a thought for rules,
Just joyful spirits and two little fools.

So join the echoes, let's shout it clear,
For laughter was our secret sphere.
In the halls of memory, we'll hold on tight,
To giggles that linger, morning to night.

Chasing Shadows in the Twilight

In twilight's glow, we rise and run,
Chasing shadows, oh what fun!
Silly shapes begin to loom,
Haunting forms in the evening gloom.

Met monsters with socks upon their heads,
Dancing on rooftops, tales like threads.
A ghostly laugh, a playful chase,
Twilight mischief, that's our space.

Tall tales spun from flickering light,
Every shadow holds a delight.
Who knew old trees could twist and prance?
Our giggled fears, a childlike dance.

So, let's embrace the silly fright,
When shadows waltz in the soft moonlight.
In every twist, we'll find our way,
Chasing shadows, what a play!

Pathways to Yesterday's Dreams

In a closet, time forgot,
Old socks dance without a thought.
They giggle and twirl, what a sight,
Making laundry day feel light.

A teddy bear with one glass eye,
Swaps tales of flying pies in the sky.
He claims to be a pirate bold,
With a treasure chest of stories untold.

Old records spin, they start to sing,
Of awkward moves and silly bling.
Remembering the days of carefree grace,
When every fall felt like a race.

In this mirthful, quirky space,
Where echoes of laughter find their place,
We chase our shadows, not in fright,
But in jest, from morn till night.

Whispers Beneath the Surface

A rubber duck, with a quack so loud,
Makes waves amidst a silent crowd.
It tells of dreams in the tub so bright,
Of bubble baths and splashes at night.

Inside the fridge, a pickle winks,
Recalling parties and kitchen kinks.
It sways to tunes of a bygone cheer,
While leftover pizza sheds a tear.

The goldfish in its bowl does twirl,
Spinning tales of an underwater whirl.
It chuckles at tales of a fishing line,
While a hungry cat makes its design.

In this realm where memories peek,
Laughter lingers, and moments speak.
The humor we find in the ordinary,
Turns whispers into things quite legendary.

The Space Between Our Words

In a book with pages worn and frayed,
Lies laughter that never fades.
It whispers jokes from long ago,
In puns and riddles, a glorious show.

With crayons strewn, a masterpiece glows,
A doodle of cats dressed in bows.
They argue and play in a silly way,
Holding court in a child's ballet.

A shadow creeps, but it's just a shoe,
That reminisces when life was new.
It thinks it's a monster, a fearsome beast,
Yet it makes us laugh, a joyful feast.

Between the lines of chatty dreams,
Lies humor dripping like melted creams.
For in those pauses, laughter flows,
Creating echoes wherever it goes.

Distant Stars of Forgotten Nights

In the attic, items piled high,
A typewriter dreams of tales to fly.
It clacks and clatters with stories bold,
Of knights who wore pajamas, or so I'm told.

Old photographs with smiles askew,
Reveal fashion faux pas and hairstyles askew.
They chuckle at poses once so grand,
And the awkwardness no one planned.

A lonely guitar hums its blues,
Composed by the memories it can't refuse.
With every strum, it plays a past tune,
That echoes below the silly moon.

From dusty corners, laughter peeks,
In whispered tales that joyfully speaks.
For those distant stars on velvet nights,
Hold the folly of our delighting sights.

Reveries of what Could Have Been

In the attic, old hats we find,
Dancing alone, quite unrefined.
A rabbit in a top hat yawns,
While the clock keeps ticking on and on.

What if we'd flown on a pink balloon?
To a party held by a raccoon?
Cake made of clouds, and lemonade streams,
Life's just a series of whimsical dreams.

We ponder on journeys we'd never take,
Like swimming in soup or riding a snake.
Imaginary friends with silly names,
Always plotting their hilarious games.

Yet here we are, in a room tucked tight,
With echoes of laughter that feel just right.
We savor the folly, the laughs shared round,
In memories made, our joy is found.

Fleeting Footsteps in the Hall

Tiptoeing through the shadows, we play,
Silent little ninjas, hip hip hooray!
The creaky floorboards join in the fun,
While we giggle at hiding from everyone.

A ghost with no manners floats on by,
Stealing my chips, oh what a sly guy!
How dare he munch on my popcorn stash,
Chasing him down, a comical clash!

In the hallway, we find a lost sock,
Its other half locked in some funny block.
Amidst the mayhem and playful shouts,
We treasure these moments, without a doubt.

The whispers of mischief linger still,
Rendering our hearts with a playful thrill.
For in every corner and light-hearted call,
Are memories waiting, should you heed their thrall.

Echoes Beneath the Surface

Beneath the surface of my old goldfish,
Lies a world of bubbles—my secret wish.
Where barnacles dance and crabs play chess,
Unruly seaweed, oh what a mess!

They laugh at humans, who flail and flop,
While eating gummy worms, non-stop.
Chasing each other in circles wide,
Everyone's invited to this wacky ride.

Occasionally, a bubble pops near,
They salute the surface with a cheer.
A dopey seal joins the party too,
With a hat made of kelp, just for view.

So if you hear echoes that make you giggle,
Know it's my fish friends, doing the jiggle.
Life's beneath the waves, all so absurd,
Filled with laughter that's rarely heard.

When Time Stood Still

In a world where clocks forgot to tick,
We'd ride on a snail, oh so quick.
With candies raining from pink cotton skies,
In a land where no kid ever cries.

We'd slide down rainbows, surf on the breeze,
Chat with the daisies and tickle the trees.
Here, gravity bends to our funny whims,
And bubbles burst forth in joyous hymns.

Yet time creeps back with a sneaky grin,
Dragging the laughter, oh where to begin?
But in our hearts, those moments stay,
When silliness ruled, and toys had their say.

So let's hold on to that timeless cheer,
A world of wonders, forever near.
For in our memories, it all shines bright,
Every silly thought, a pure delight.

Scenes from a Faded Past

We danced like spaghetti, under the moonlight,
With moves that resembled a cat's shaky fight.
The neighbors all chuckled, we didn't care,
Our feet seemed to float, just light as the air.

The pizza we ordered, a tower of cheese,
Carried by dreams and our youthful ease.
We laughed 'til we cried, at that old hat's look,
But tragically, forgot how to read the book.

We stomped through the park, with music so loud,
Making up lyrics and feeling so proud.
With every short coming, a high-five was due,
We told ourselves tales, like a sitcom crew.

So here's to the moments we made so absurd,
Each slip, trip, and tumble, a slapstick word.
Let's raise our glasses to those misfit days,
And smile at the chaos our memory plays.

Whispers of Our Lost Hopes

We set out to conquer and travel the world,
But lost our map, like a flag unfurled.
The train we missed? Oh, that's rich!
We stowed our dreams in a little old pitch.

Hopes as big as balloons, they floated away,
With heights we imagined, they chose to delay.
We giggled at plans that never took flight,
Just grounded our laughter toward the night.

We tried to be grown-ups but ended with pies,
On our faces, not plates, were the biggest surprise.
With aprons and spatulas, things went awry,
Who knew cooking would surely make us cry?

But every mishap became a great tale,
Of adventures gone wrong, we'd laugh and we'd wail.
Let's toast once again to our youthful mistakes,
Two clowns in the circus, avoiding the stakes.

Reflections in a Dusty Mirror

Caught glimpses of us, in the glassy sheen,
With hair all askew, looking rather obscene.
The hairstyles we sported, a trendway disaster,
Faded like memes, oh, they went by faster.

Bright colors and shapes that looked so bizarre,
Winking at selfies, we were quite the star.
Fashion faux pas? We embraced all the fray,
In a glittery riot, we danced 'til the day.

Our thoughts in a jangle, a ring of flutes,
With serious faces, we tried on suits.
Yet laughter would burst, breaking all norms,
Like kittens in tuxedos, amidst the storms.

So let's raise our glasses to memories clear,
In that dusty old mirror, we faced our own cheer.
For every reflection, a grin would ensure,
That misfit adventures make living a cure.

Notes from an Abandoned Heart

Once penned love letters that led to a crush,
But ended in doodles, a humorous hush.
Who knew that the heart had a mind of its own?
It danced on the page, like a puppy alone.

Our grand plans for love soon turned into jest,
With awkward first dates, we truly felt blessed.
Spilling our drinks while toasting a dream,
Falling off chairs, just part of the scheme.

Time turned our romances to breakfast delights,
With eggs that exploded in kitchen fights.
We laughed at the past, what a theatrical play,
Where hearts were just actors, trailing away.

So here's to the scribbles, the laughter, the flair,
The notes of our hearts, just floating in air.
With every misstep, another tale spun,
Our comedy lives on, in the fading sun.

The Quiet Between Heartbeats

In the silence where laughter hides,
Old memories dance in funny strides.
Like socks that lost their match at play,
They trip on echoes, bright and gray.

A sandwich left at lunch's start,
Stares back like a forgotten art.
With mustard swirls and crumbs galore,
It whispers tales of days before.

When time was measured by the laughs,
And every joke drew crazy graphs.
In the pauses, joy found its height,
Like shadows playing tag at night.

So hold your breath, let giggles sprout,
In spaces where fears fade out.
The quirks of life, in hues so sweet,
Bring chuckles that dance on nimble feet.

Resilience of Yesterday's Echoes

Old shoes sit by the door, so worn,
They tell of trips both lost and borne.
Each scuff a tale, a twist, a turn,
In laughter's glow, we brightly burn.

With spilled drinks and silly slips,
Here we stumble, share our quips.
A mirror bent reflects our grins,
Of bloopers where each story spins.

In the garden of our blunders,
Life's humor waits like summer thunders.
Just when you think you've found the prize,
A noodle slips, oh how life flies!

Resilient hearts, they bounce right back,
With giggles hiding in the cracks.
We toast to moments filled with cheer,
And twirl in shadows without fear.

Fables of Forgotten Paths

Once upon a time, it seemed,
Life was a prank—we all dreamed.
With twists and turns and tales bizarre,
We chased our futures, never far.

A cat that slipped on garden walls,
Was king of merry, feline brawls.
In every giggle, wisdom grows,
Through silly steps, the laughter flows.

Old bikes with flat tires cluttered lanes,
Whisper secrets of youth's refrains.
Every fall a story forged,
In laughter's light, our spirits gorged.

So gather now, let's spin a yarn,
Of fables bright, of spirits warm.
In forgotten paths, the fun persists,
As joy's embrace, we can't resist.

The Prism of Past Encounters

Memories bounce like light through glass,
Reflecting moments, they quickly pass.
In every color, a giggle grows,
A spectrum of funny, daring prose.

Forgotten hats on heads they sway,
With mismatched shoes that lead astray.
In joyful chaos, we lose our way,
But laughter's compass saves the day.

Old friends appear in strange new forms,
With stories wrapped in playful norms.
In the prism, we find the spark,
That lights our paths when days grow dark.

So let us toast with goofy grins,
To past encounters, where the fun begins.
With every misstep, we rise, we play,
In the dance of time, we find our way.

Reflections of a Withered Bloom

In a vase, I sit alone,
Memories tangled like weeds have grown.
Once bright and bold, now dusty and gray,
In my floral past, I danced every day.

My petals fell, but who would know?
I'll tell the tales of the once vibrant show.
A sprinkle of water, a dash of good cheer,
Yet here I reside, with a wizard's beard, dear.

The bees used to buzz, the sun shone so bright,
I was the life of every garden night.
But now I just charm the curious ants,
Who come for the gossip, not for the plants.

So here I ponder, in silence I bloom,
With every lost moment still lighting my room.
The laughter of pollen that once filled the air,
Is echoed in shadows and dust everywhere.

When We Were Younger

Remember the swings and the way we soared?
With every push, our giggles roared.
Knees scraped and laughter, we flew up high,
Oh, to be kids again, or at least to try!

We traded our toys for the latest craze,
Running wild in the sunshine haze.
Now we sit here, in shirts with stains,
Chasing memories down the amusement lanes.

Ice cream drips and a belly full of fries,
Those carefree days were quite the surprise.
Now we chuckle at photos in piles,
Embarrassed by fashion, but oh, the smiles!

When we were young, oh so carefree,
The world was a canvas, as grand as could be.
Now we just watch our kids take the stage,
With a wink and a nod, we turn the page.

The Light That Once Shone

In the attic, I found an old puppet on strings,
He danced in the light where the laughter still clings.
We pulled on those threads, oh, what a delight,
Frolicking fervently, all day and all night.

A flashlight in hand, we explored every nook,
Reading secrets from an adventure-filled book.
Now it's just dust and a tattered old shawl,
But that glow in our hearts still remembers it all.

Those candles of joy that flickered so bright,
Now dimmed by the years and the noise of the night.
Yet when I turn down the world's raucous tone,
I can still feel those sparkles, that light we owned.

And though we have aged, and shadows may creep,
The light of the past still makes me leap.
For every old laugh and each whimsical play,
Lives on in the echoes that refuse to decay.

Reverberations of Distant Laughter

Echoes remind me of days gone by,
When laughter erupted, oh my, oh my!
We played pranks on the neighbors, a riotous spree,
Yet here in my chair, it's just ghosts, you see.

With mischief and glee, we hopped on our bikes,
Racing the shadows, not caring for spikes.
Now I sip tea, while the children pass by,
With giggles like thunder, they soar to the sky.

Flashes of summers, the water balloon fight,
Rules didn't matter, oh, what a delight!
My soggy old memories make me guffaw,
As I watch youngsters create mayhem, no law!

So I chuckle and muse on these echoes so dear,
The laughter of youth, now ringing quite clear.
Though time marches on, its footsteps may clatter,
The joy stays alive in the cracks, hearts still chatter.

Faded Ink of Our Lovelorn Sonnets

In the drawer lies love notes, neglected,
The ink feels faint, like a ghost who defected.
Hearts once aflame, now a dusty affair,
Whispers of laughter linger in the air.

Starlit promises scribbled in haste,
Now read with a chuckle, their glory replaced.
Who knew sweet nothings could turn out so funny?
A love that was rich now feels rather punny.

We danced with abandon, made silly mistakes,
Like tripping on shoelaces, or breaking our fakes.
Lost in the rhythm of awkward romance,
Who knew that romance came with a dance?

Beneath all the sighs, a tickle remains,
An echo of joy through our stubborn refrains.
So let's toast to the jesters of love's old lore,
With laughter and wine, we'll forget what's in store.

Unraveled Dreams in the Winds of Change

Kites once so high, now tangled in trees,
They laugh at our efforts, like ungrateful bees.
Dreams that we nurtured have flown off the stage,
What once felt like magic now feels like a cage.

Plans laid out neatly with care and precision,
Only to crumble, what a grand decision!
We juggled our hopes, like a clown on a spree,
The circus we've built isn't just about glee.

Who thought our future could twist like a maze,
With maps full of detours, confounding displays?
Yet here we are smiling, despite all the mess,
Finding humor in chaos, isn't life such a jest?

The wind plays tricks, swirling dreams like confetti,
With laughter as fuel, we'll stay light and ready.
So let's dance with the breeze and embrace the surprise,
In the carnival of life, we'll wear goofball ties.

Reverberations of Old Promises

Echoes of vows slip through time's gentle hands,
We promised forever with chalk on soft sands.
Now we're left chuckling at dreams that once soared,
Reasoning with laughter, our hopes were ignored.

Like a bad magician, we pulled out our hearts,
Only to find they'd been lost at the marts.
We said 'I do' with cupcakes and cheer,
Who knew our romance would turn into beer?

Old love letters stacked high, now collectibles rare,
Laughter erupts from the things we laid bare.
With each silly promise that felt ever so true,
The punchline of fate is just me and you.

So here's to the echoes, each giggle and sigh,
To all of the moments we shared with a pie.
We'll always remember our whimsical past,
With grins on our faces, forever steadfast.

The Color of Distant Echoes

Memories painted in hues of pure fun,
Splashy adventures under the sun.
The laughter we shared, bright like a hue,
Faded but vivid in hearts that still grew.

Silly selfies and memes that once ruled,
Time played a trick and our hearts bloomed.
The gallery of maybes, a comedic affair,
Life's a sitcom, with jokes everywhere.

We'll frame all the blunders that make us feel whole,
Tales of our mischief, they brighten the soul.
With laughter as brushstrokes, we capture the day,
Creating a canvas where joy leads the way.

So let's color our lives with all that we've gained,
With witticisms shared, and laughter unchained.
For the echoes of us will always stay bright,
Like a midnight giggle wrapped snugly in light.

The Weight of Silent Thoughts

In shadows cast by idle dreams,
A funny dance of whispered schemes.
Where giggles hide in crumpled pages,
And laughter echoes through the stages.

With heavy hearts and lightened feet,
We stumble through this awkward feat.
Each thought floats by like buttered toast,
We chuckle softly at our ghost.

In corners where regrets reside,
We poke at them, we joke, we bide.
For every sigh that slips away,
A punchline helps to save the day.

So raise a glass to fleeting thoughts,
To all the laughs that time forgot.
We'll toast to all those silent screams,
And dance amidst our wobbly dreams.

Frayed Edges of a Well-Worn Tale

Once upon a time, they say,
A tale got lost along the way.
With frayed edges and crooked lines,
It tickles us as history whines.

Through mishaps and a lopsided grin,
We trip through all the yarns of sin.
Each memory's like a comic strip,
We laugh so hard, we lose our grip.

Old heroes in their tattered capes,
Wielding spoons instead of drapes.
Their battles fought with silly quotes,
Defending honor with rubber boats.

So gather round and share a laugh,
At every slip in our dear path.
For every fable that feels frail,
Hides a treasure, a funny tale.

Ephemeral Echoes of Lost Time

Tick-tock goes the sneaky clock,
As memories tease and time just mocks.
With each swirl and playful twist,
We chase the moments that we've missed.

Like bubbles bursting, bright and fleeting,
Our minds are busy with retreating.
In every chuckle, a glance is tossed,
In laughter found, it's never lost.

We reminisce on silly days,
With mismatched socks and wacky ways.
Our past is a circus, a wild ride,
Where clowns are cherished, and we abide.

So here's to echoes that cease to chime,
To the merry mess of lost time.
In every giggle, we reclaim,
The joy of living without shame.

Through the Veil of Forgotten Love

Behind a curtain, love takes flight,
In funny shades of wrong and right.
With tangled hearts and mismatched shoes,
We wade through sentiments we choose.

A wink here, a sigh there,
Adventures sprinkle everywhere.
Like silly goose, we tiptoe round,
Creating swirls of laughter bound.

In every glance, a memory peeks,
The jokes of time in silly streaks.
We stumble on our heartfelt notes,
While harmony hums on quirky boats.

So let's embrace the love that fades,
In goofy ways through memory's shades.
For every whimsy, a giggle's born,
Through laughter's lens, new love is worn.

Silhouettes of a Distant Now

In shadows where our laughter fades,
We trip on jokes that time parades.
Each snicker caught like cupboard dust,
A memory framed in 'happened once.'

We sipped on dreams from goofy cups,
And danced with socks, forgetting clums.
Life played tricks and we played back,
With silent giggles on the track.

Memories Wrapped in Silk

A wrap of silk, hugs of bright cheer,
We channel our past, but not with fear.
In quilts of mishaps, we muster glee,
While squirrels mock us in a tree.

Cartwheels into Mondays, don't ask why,
Our hairstyles stuck like a fly.
We frame our whims on a dusty shelf,
Encouraging chuckles from our younger self.

Lurking in Our Yesterday

With playful pants and oversized shoes,
We peek at mornings, spreading blues.
Those daring stunts, a trip, a fall,
We laugh at life, heedless of it all.

Oh, the blunders that made us wise,
Like misplaced wigs and goofy pies.
Our past, a riddle, a jigsaw dance,
In funny hats, we take a chance.

Phantoms of the Unlived Life

Bouncing like rubber from dream to dream,
We ride our blunders like a wild stream.
There's a charm in things we never tried,
In chubby costumes, we laugh, we hide.

Silly moments haunt our snazzy paths,
Like dancing doormats that avoid baths.
Yet bright spirits linger, teasing and spry,
In the wacky tales that never die.

The Sound of Our Unsaid Goodbyes

In a room full of laughter, we slip like a cue,
Words hang in the air, but they're stuck like glue.
We wave with a smile, then we trip on our feet,
Like penguins on ice, we can't find the beat.

The clock strikes a pose, and we fumble with time,
Counting the seconds like it's a weird rhyme.
We share knowing glances, with secrets to keep,
While giggles erupt like we're kids, half-asleep.

Each sigh is a song, each glance is a thread,
Tangled in memories that tickle our head.
So we keep saying nothing, just nod and we grin,
As if silence were gold, so we're destined to win.

When the curtains draw close, and we're stuck in our chairs,
We chuckle at moments and odd little stares.
Our unsaid goodbyes dance in mischief and mirth,
As echoes of laughter keep haunting our hearth.

Pages Torn by Time's Hand

We leaf through the pages, they flutter and sigh,
Each tear tells a joke, we just can't comply.
The story gets squished, like a sandwich too tight,
And time, in its haste, turns both day and night.

Crumbs of our laughter fall out on the floor,
As we juggle the past, while keeping the score.
With every new chapter, the plot plays a game,
Characters change, but we still feel the same.

Our memories flit like they're trapped in a breeze,
Each one a page that just begs to appease.
But oh, how they shine, even when they're all bent,
Like letters from grandmas, their love's evident.

So here's to the tales that we can't quite retrieve,
To the sentences mangled yet still, we believe.
We're scribes for our memories, in laughter we stand,
Turning pages together, like flowers in hand.

The Remembrance of Youth's Glow

In the mirror's reflection, a wink from the past,
Where the frames of our youth fit us far too fast.
With giggles like raindrops, we frolic and play,
Chasing shadows of daydreams that giggle away.

We wore silly hats and danced with great flair,
Each moment a treasure, like candy to share.
The clocks all conspired, they spun on a whim,
In a world where we flourished, no reason to swim.

Our nostalgia is funny, like socks with no pairs,
Each thread holds a story, like unkempt hair stares.
With laughter as fuel, we ride on this train,
As we echo those memories wrapped up in a chain.

So here's to bright cheeks and to silly charades,
We script our own tales, taking bets on the trades.
In youth's golden glow, let's forever be free,
With giggles as lanterns, let mischief decree.

Where Memories Dance in Shadows

Under the moonlight, where shadows all sway,
Our memories shimmy, they leap into play.
Footloose and fancy, they tango so bright,
While we sit and chuckle at the capers of night.

With each silly mishap, our laughter's a song,
As the tales of our past think they still belong.
Like socks in the dryer, all tangled and spun,
We weave through the chaos, and we call it fun.

In the corners, we find little moments left dear,
A slip of the tongue or a burst of a cheer.
As we dance with our echoes, each spin's a delight,
Chasing time in a whirl, it'll be alright.

So come join the shadows and sway to the beat,
With whispers and giggles, our stories repeat.
In the dance of our lives, let's step without care,
For the shadows will hush, as we float in midair.

www.ingramcontent.com/pod-product-compliance
Ingram Content Group UK Ltd.
Pitfield, Milton Keynes, MK11 3LW, UK
UKHW022149231224
452890UK00011B/410